MW00412413

DRINKING

Because you are but a young man, beware of temptations and snares; and above all, be careful to keep yourself in the use of means; resort to good company; and howbeit you be nicknamed a Puritan, and mocked, yet care not for that, but rejoice and be glad, that they who are scorned and scoffed by this godless and vain world, and nicknamed Puritans, would admit you to their society; for I must tell you, when I am at this point as you see me, I get no comfort to my soul by any second means under heaven but from those who are nicknamed Puritans. They are the men that can give a word of comfort to a wearied soul in due season, and that I have found by experience . . .

THE LAST AND HEAVENLY SPEECHES, AND
GLORIOUS DEPARTURE, OF JOHN, VISCOUNT KENMURE

BINGE
DRINKING

John Flavel

Taken from
'A Caution to Seamen: A Dissuasive against
Several Horrid and Detestable Sins',
The Works of John Flavel, Vol. 5

Also includes an extract from C. H. Spurgeon's
John Ploughman's Pictures

THE BANNER OF TRUTH TRUST

THE BANNER OF TRUTH TRUST
3 Murrayfield Road, Edinburgh EH12 6EL, UK
P.O. Box 621, Carlisle, PA 17013, USA

*

© The Banner of Truth Trust 2008

ISBN-978 1 84871 015 3

*

Typeset in 10.5 / 13.5 pt Adobe Caslon Pro
at the Banner of Truth Trust, Edinburgh

Printed in the USA by
Versa Press, Inc.,
East Peoria, IL

*

Minor editorial adjustments have been made to the
original text, e.g. the modernizing of some words
and the supply of Scripture references.

BINGE DRINKING

*I*n the former treatise[1] I have endeavoured to spiritualize earthly objects, and elevate your thoughts to more sublime and excellent contemplations; that earthly things may rather be a step, than a stop to heavenly. You have therein my best advice to guide you in your course to that port of your eternal rest and happiness.

[1] *A New Compass for Seamen: or, Navigation Spiritualized*, see *Works*, vol. 5, pp. 206-93, *Ed.*

In this I have given warning of some dangerous rocks and quicksands that lie upon your left hand; upon which millions of souls have perished, and others are wilfully running to their own perdition. Such are the horrid sins of *drunkenness, uncleanness,*[2] *profane swearing, violation of promises, engagements made to God, and atheistical slighting and contempt of death and eternity.* All which I have here given warning of, and held forth a light to discover where your danger is. If after this you obstinately prosecute your lusts, and will not be reclaimed, you perish without apology, I have freed mine own soul.

Let none interpret this necessary plainness as a reproach to seamen, as if I

---

[2] See *Impure Lust,* another title by John Flavel in the Pocket Puritan series published by the Trust, *Ed.*

represented them to the world worse than they are. If, upon that account, any of them be offended, I think these three or four considerations should remove that offence.

First, that if this close and plain dealing be necessary, in order to your cure, and you will be offended by it, it is better *you* should be offended than *God.* Ministers are often put upon lamentable straits, they sail between Scylla and Charybdis—the wrath of God upon one side, if we do not speak plain and home, as the necessity of the case requires, and man's wrath if we do. What shall we do in this strait? Either God or you, it seems, must be offended; and if it cannot be avoided, I shall rather hazard your anger than God's, and think it far more tolerable.

Secondly, If you did but see the necessity and end of this manner of dealing with your souls, you would not be offended. But put it into a more sensible case, and you will see and acknowledge it presently. If I should see an high-built wall giving way, and ready to fall upon you, would you be angry with me, if by plucking you out of the danger, I should pluck your arm out of joint? Certainly you would not. Why, this is the case here: See Isaiah 30:13: 'Therefore this iniquity shall be to you as a breach ready to fall, swelling out in a high wall, whose breaking cometh suddenly, at an instant.'

Thirdly, What a madness is it to abide in a condition over which all woes and curses hang, and yet not be able to endure to hear about it! Why, what will it profit you to have your misery hid from your eyes, and kept from your ears a little while? You must see this wrath, and hear louder volleys of woes from your own consciences, if you remain in this condition. You cannot bear that from us, which your conscience will one of these days preach themselves to you, and that in a more dreadful dialect than I have used here.

Fourthly, I do not charge these sins indifferently upon all seamen. No, I know there are some choice and good men amongst your men, that fear an oath, and hate even the garments spotted with the flesh, who are (I question not) the credit and glory of our English nation, in the eyes of strangers that converse with them. Nor yet do I think that all that are wicked amongst them are equally guilty of all these evils; for though all that are graceless be equally under the dominion of original corruption, yet it follows not from thence, that therefore actual sins must reign alike in them: there is a great difference, even among ungodly men themselves in this respect; which difference arises from their various customs, constitutions, abilities, educations, and the different administrations of the Spirit, in enlightening, convincing, and putting checks upon conscience: for though God be not the author, yet he is the orderer of sin. And this makes a great disparity, even among wicked men themselves. Some are persons of good morals, though not gracious principles, which produce a civil and sober, though not a holy and religious life. And others, though they live in some one of these lusts, yet are not guilty of some others of them.

For it is with original corruption, just as it is with the sap of the earth, which though it be the matter of all kind of fruits, yet in some ground it sorts better with one grain than with another: and so in plants, in one tree it becomes an apple, in another a cherry; even so it is with this original corruption, in one man it runs most into swearing, in another into uncleanness, in a third into drunkenness. Lust is nothing else but the corrupt appetite of the creature to some sinful object; and therefore look as it is with the appetite with respect to food, so it is with the vitiated appetites of souls to sin. One man loves this food best, and another that; there is endless variety in that, and so in this.

Having spoken thus much to remove offence, I shall now beg you to peruse the following discourse. Consider what evidence these things carry with them. Search the alleged scriptures, see if they be truly recited and applied to the case in hand: And if so, O tremble at the truth you read and bring forth your lusts, that they may die the death! Will you not part with these abominable practices till death and hell make the separation? Ah! how much better is it for you that grace should do it? And because many of you see not the danger, and therefore prize not the remedy, I do here request all those that have the heart of pity in them, for their poor relations, who are sinking, drowning, perishing, to spread these following cautions before the Lord for a blessing, and then put them into their hands. And O that all pious masters would persuade all those that are under their charge to buy this ensuing treatise, and diligently peruse it.

Beware of the Detestable Sin of Drunkenness

Take heed, and beware of the detestable sin of drunkenness, which is a beastly sin, a voluntary madness, a sin that unmans you, and makes you like the beasts that perish; yea, sets you below the beasts, which will not drink to excess; or, if they do, yet it is not their sin. One of the ancients calls it

A distemper of the head, a subversion of the senses, a tempest in the tongue, a storm of the body, the shipwreck of virtue, the loss of time, a wilful madness, a pleasant devil, a sugared poison, a sweet sin, which he that has, has not himself, and he that commits it, does not only commit sin, but he himself is altogether sin.

It is a sin at which the most sober heathens blushed. The Spartans brought their children to loathe it, by showing them a drunkard, whom they gazed at as a monster: even Epicurus himself, who esteemed happiness to consist in pleasure, yet was temperate, as Cicero observes. Among the heathens he was accounted the best man that spent more oil in the lamp than wine in the bottle. Christianity could once glory in its professors: Tertullian says of the primitive Christians, they sat not down before they prayed; they ate no more than might suffice hunger, they drank no more than was sufficient for temperate men; they did so eat and drink, as those that remembered they must pray afterward. But now we may blush to behold such beastly sensualists adorning themselves with its name, and sheltering themselves under its wings.

And amongst those that profess Christianity, how ordinarily is this sin committed by seamen? This insatiable dropsy is a disease that reigns, especially among the inferior and ruder sort of them. Some of them have gone aboard drunk, and laid the foundation of their voyage in sin. O what a preparation is this! They know not whether ever they shall see the land of their nativity any more: the next storm may send them into eternity: yet this is the farewell they take, this is their preparation to meet the Lord. And so in their returns, notwithstanding the terrible and astonishing works of the Lord, which they have beheld with their eyes, and their marvellous preservation in so great and terrible extremities; yet thus do they requite the Lord, as soon as their dangers are over, as if they had been delivered to commit all these abominations.

But a few hours or days since, they were reeling to and fro upon a stormy ocean, and staggering like drunken men, as it is said in Psalm 107:27; and now you may see them reeling and staggering in the streets, drowning the sense of all those precious mercies and deliverances in their drunken cups.

Reader, if you be one that is guilty of this sin, for the Lord's sake think about yourself speedily, and weigh, with the reason of a man, what I shall now say, in order to your conviction, humiliation, and reformation.

I need not spend many words, to open the nature of this sin to you; we all grant, that there is a lawful use of wine and strong drink to support nature, not to clog it; to cure infirmities, not to cause them. 'Drink no longer water, but use a little wine, for thy stomach's sake, and thine often infirmities', says Paul to Timothy (1 *Tim.* 5:23). Mark, drink not water, but wine; *Sed modice,* (i.e.) *medice: pro remedio, non pro deliciis,* says Ambrose; that is, use it modestly, *viz.* medicinally, not for pleasure, but for remedy. Yea, God allows it, not only for bare necessity, but for cheerfulness and alacrity, that the body may be more fit and more expedite for duty (*Prov.* 31 :7), but further no man proceeds, without the violation of sobriety. When men sit till wine have inflamed them, and reason be disturbed, (for drunkenness is the privation of reason, caused by immoderate drinking), then do they come under the guile of this horrid and abominable sin. To the satisfaction and refreshment of nature, you may drink; for it is a part of the curse to drink, and not be satisfied; but take heed and go no further; 'For wine is a mocker, strong drink is raging, and whosoever is deceived thereby, is not wise' (*Prov.* 20:1).

The throat is a slippery place; how easily may a sin slip through it into the soul? These sensual pleasures have a kind of enchanting power upon the soul, and by custom gain upon it, till they have enslaved it, and brought it under their power.

Now, this is the sin against which God has delivered so many precepts, and denounced so many woes, in his Word:

Be not drunken with wine, wherein is excess (*Eph.* 5:18);

Not in rioting and drunkenness, not in chambering and wantonness (*Rom.* 13:13);

Woe to them that rise up early in the morning, that they may follow strong drink, that continue until night, till wine inflame them (*Isa.* 5:11),

with many other of dreadful importance.

Now, to startle you for ever from this abominable and filthy lust, I shall here propound to your consideration these ten ensuing arguments; and O that they might stand in the way, as the angel did in Balaam's, when you are in the prosecution of your sensual pleasures! And the first is this:

ARGUMENT 1.

It should exceedingly dissuade from this sin, to consider that it is an high abuse of the bounty and goodness of God in affording us those sweet refreshments, to make our lives comfortable to us upon earth.

In Adam we forfeited all right to all earthly as well as heavenly mercies. God might have taken you from the womb, when you were a sinner but of a span long, and immediately have sent you to your own place. You had no right to a drop of water more than what the bounty of God gave you: and whereas he might have thrust you out of the world as soon as you came into it, and so all those days of mercy you have had on earth might have been spent in howling and unspeakable misery in hell—behold the bounty and goodness of God to you.

I say, behold it, and wonder! He has suffered you for so many years to live upon the earth, which he has prepared and furnished with all things fit for your necessity and delight: out of the earth, on which you tread, 'he bringeth forth thy food, and wine to make glad thy heart' (*Psa.* 104:14-15). And do you thus requite the Lord? Has mercy armed an enemy to fight against it with its own weapons? Ah! that ever the riches of his goodness, bounty, and longsuffering, all which are arguments to lead you to repentance, should be thus abused! If God had not been so bountiful, you could not have been so sinful.

ARGUMENT 2.

It degrades a man from the honour of his creation, and equalizes him to the beast that perishes: wine is said to take away the heart (Hos. 4:11), i.e. the wisdom and ingenuity of a man, and so brutifies him, as Nebuchadnezzar, who lost the heart of a man and had the heart of a beast given him (Dan. 4:32).

The heart of a man has its generosity and sprightliness—brave, vigorous spirits in it, capable of, and fitted for noble and worthy actions and employments—but his lust effeminates, quenches, and drowns that masculine vigour in the puddle of excess and sensuality: for no sooner is a man brought under the dominion of this lust, but the government of reason is renounced, which should exercise a coercive power over the affections, and all is delivered up into the hands of lust and appetite: and so they act not by discretion and reason, but by lust and will, as the beasts do by instinct.

The spirit of man entertains itself with intellectual and chaste delights; the soul of a beast is only fitted for such low, sensitive, and dreggy pleasures. You have something of the *angel*, and something of the *beast* in you; your soul partakes of the nature of angels, your body of the nature of beasts. Oh! how many pamper the *beast* while they starve the *angel*?

God, in the first chapter [of Genesis], put all the creatures in subjection to you; by this lust you put yourself in subjection to the creature, and are brought under its power (1 *Cor.* 6:12). If God had given you the head or feet of a beast, O! what a misery would you have esteemed it? And is it nothing to have the heart of a beast? O! consider it sadly.

ARGUMENT 3.

It is a sin by which you greatly wrong and abuse your own body.

The body is the soul's instrument; it is as the tools are to a skilful artificer. This lust both dulls and spoils it, so that it is utterly unfit for any service of him that made it.

Your body is a curious piece, not made by a word of command, as other creatures, but by a word of counsel; 'I am fearfully and wonderfully made, and curiously wrought', says the Psalmist, (*Psa.* 139:14-15), or as the vulgar, *Acupictus sum,* Painted as with needle-work of diverse colours, like a garment richly embroidered. Look how many members, so many wonders! There are miracles enough, says one, between head and foot to fill a volume. There is, says another, such curious workmanship in the eye, that upon the first sight of it, some Atheists have been forced to acknowledge a God; especially that fifth muscle in the eye is wonderful, whereby, (as a learned author observes) man differs from all other creatures, who have but four; one to turn the eye downward, a second to hold it forward, a third to move it to the right-hand, a fourth to the left; but none to turn it upward as a man has.

Now, judge in yourself; did God frame such a curious piece, and enliven it with a soul, which is a spark, a ray of his own light, whose motions are so quick, various, and indefatigable, whose flights of reason are so transcendent; did God, do you think, send down this curious piece, the top and glory of the creation, the *index* and *epitome* of the whole world, did God, I say, send down this picture of his own perfection, to be but as a strainer for meats and drinks, a sponge to suck in wine and beer?

Or can you answer for the abuse and destruction of it? By this excess you fill it with innumerable diseases, under which it languishes; and at last your life, like a lamp, is extinguished, being drowned with too much oil. 'Infinite diseases are begotten by it, (says Zanchius); hence comes apoplexies, gouts, palsies, sudden death, trembling of the hands and legs'; herein they bring Cain's curse upon themselves, says Ambrose: drunkenness slays more than a sword. Oh! what a terrible thing will it be to consider upon a death-bed, that these pangs and aches are the fruits of your intemperance and excess!

Who hath woe? Who hath sorrow?
Who hath contentions? Who hath
babbling? Who hath wounds without
cause? Who hath redness of eyes? They
that tarry long at the wine, they that go
to seek mixed wine (*Prov.* 23:29-30).

By this *enumeration* and manner of
interrogation, he seems to make it a difficult
thing to recount the miseries that drunkenness loads the outward man with; for look,
as vermin abound where there is store of
corn, so do diseases in the bodies of drunkards, where crudities do so abound. Now, I
think, if you have no regard to your poor
soul, or the glory of God, yet such a sensible
argument as this, from your body, should
move you.

ARGUMENT 4.

Drunkenness wastes and scatters your estate, poverty attends excess; the drunkard shall be clothed with rags, and brought to a morsel of bread.

Solomon has read your fortune, 'He that loveth wine and oil shall not be rich'; (*Prov.* 21 :17); luxury and beggary are seldom far asunder. When Diogenes heard a drunkard's house had to be sold said, 'I thought it would not be long e'er he vomited up his house also.'

The Hebrew word יודש and the Greek word ασωπα, which signifies luxury; the former is compounded of two words, which signify, *You shall be poor;* and the latter signifies the losing of the possession of that good which is in our hand. 'The drunkard and the glutton shall surely come to poverty', (*Prov.* 23:21). In the Hebrew it is, he shall be disinherited or dispossessed. It does not only dispossess a man of his reason, which is a rich and fair inheritance given to him by God, but it also dispossesses him of his estate: it wastes all that either the provident care of your progenitors, or the blessing of God upon your own industry, has obtained for you.

And how will this sting like an adder, when you shall consider it? Apicus the Roman, hearing that there were seven hundred crowns only remaining of a fair estate that his father had left him, fell into a deep melancholy, and fearing want, hanged himself, says Seneca. And not to mention the miseries and sorrows they bring hereby upon their families, drinking the tears, yea, the blood of their wives and children: Oh! what an account will they give to God, when the reckoning day comes! Believe it, Sirs, there is not a shilling of your estates, but God will reckon with you for the expense thereof. If you have spent it upon your lusts, whilst the necessity of your families, or the poor, called upon you for it, I should be loathe to have your account to make, for a thousand times more than ever you possessed. O woeful expense, that is followed with such dreadful reckonings!

Argument 5.

Consider what vile and ignominious characters the Spirit of God has put upon the subjects of this sin.

The Scripture everywhere notes them for infamous, and most abominable persons. When Eli supposed Hannah to be drunken, 'Count not thine handmaid a daughter of Belial', said she, (1 *Sam.* 1:16). Now, a son or daughter of Belial is, in Scripture-language, the vilest of men or women. So Psalm 69:12: 'They that sit in the gate, speak against me, and I am the song of drunkards', i.e. of the basest and vilest of men, as the opposition plainly shows; for they are opposed to them that sit in the gate, that is honourable persons. The Lord would have his people shun the society of such as a pest, not to eat with them, (1 *Cor.* 5:11). Yea, the Scripture brands them with atheism; they are such as have lost the sense and expectation of the day of judgment; mind not another world, nor do they look for the coming of the Lord, (*Matt.* 24:27). He says the Lord delays his coming, and then falls into drinking with the drunkard. The thoughts of that day will make them leave their cups, or their cups will drown the thoughts of such a day.

And will not all the contempt, shame and infamy which the Spirit of God has poured on the head of this sin cause you to abhor it? Do not all godly, yea, moral persons, abhor the drunkard? Oh! I think the shame that attends it, should be as a fence to keep you from it.

Argument 6.

Sadly consider, there can be nothing of the sanctifying Spirit in a soul that is under the dominion of this lust; for upon the first discovery of the grace of God, the soul renounces the government of sensuality.

'The grace of God that bringeth salvation, teacheth men to live soberly' (*Titus* 2:11-12). That is one of its first effects. Drunkenness indeed may be found among heathens who are lost in the darkness of ignorance but it may not be once named among the children of the day. 'They that be drunken, are drunken in the night; but let us that are of the day, be sober' (1 *Thess.* 5:7-8). And the apostles often oppose wine and the Spirit as things incompatible, 'Be not drunk with wine, wherein is excess; but be filled with the Spirit' (*Eph.* 5:18). So Jude 19, 'Sensual, not having the Spirit.'

Now what a dreadful consideration is this—'If any man have not the Spirit of Christ, he is none of his' (*Rom.* 8:9). Sensual persons have not the Spirit of Christ, and so can be none of his. It is true, Noah, a godly man, once fell into this sin; but, as Theodoret says, and that truly, it proceeded *ab inexperientia, non ab intemperantia*—from want of experience of the force and power of the grape, not from intemperance. And, besides, we find not that ever he was again overtaken with that sin; but you know it, and yet persist—a wretched creature!—the Spirit of Christ cannot dwell in you. The Lord help you to lay it to heart sadly!

Argument 7.

It is a sin over which many direful woes and threats hang in the word, like so many lowering clouds, ready to pour down vengeance upon the heads of such sinners.

Look, as the condition of the saints is compassed round with promises, so is yours with threatenings, 'Woe to them that rise up early in the morning, that they may follow strong drink, and continue until night, until wine inflame them' (*Isa.* 5:11). So Isaiah 28:1-2, 'Woe to the crown of pride, to the drunkards of Ephraim', &c. with many others, too long to be enumerated here. Now, consider what a fearful thing it is to be under these woes of God! Sinner, I beseech you, do not make light of them, for they will fall heavy; assure yourself not one of them shall fall to the ground; they will all take place upon you, except you repent.

There are woes of men, and woes of God: God's woes are true woes, and make their condition woeful, to purpose, on whom they fall. Other woes, as one says, do but touch the skin, but these strike the soul; other woes are but temporal, these are eternal; others do only part between us and our outward comforts, these between God and us for ever.

ARGUMENT 8.

Drunkenness is a leading sin, which has a great retinue and attendance of other sins waiting on it; it is like a sudden landflood, which brings a great deal of dirt with it.

So that look as faith excels among the graces, because it enlivens, actuates, and gives strength to them, so is this amongst sins. It is not so much a special sin against a single precept of God, as a general violation of the whole law, says accurate Amesius. It does not only call off the guard, but warms and quickens all other lusts, and so exposes the soul to be prostituted by them.

(1.) It gives occasion, yea, is the real cause of many contentions, and fatal quarrels, 'Who hath woe? Who hath sorrow? Who hath [contentions] babbling, wounds without cause? They that tarry long at the wine', &c. (*Prov.* 23:29). Contentions and wounds are the ordinary effects of drunken meetings: when reason is deposed, and lust heated, what will not men attempt?

(2.) Scoffs and reproaches of the ways and people of God, 'David was the song of the drunkards' (*Psa.* 69:12).

(3.) It is the great incendiary of lust: You shall find rioting and drunkenness joined with chambering and wantonness, (*Rom.* 13:13). *Nunquam ego ebrium castum putabo*, says Jerome—I will never think a drunkard to be chaste. Solomon plainly tells us what the issue will be, 'Thine eyes shall behold a strange woman, and thy heart shall utter perverse things', speaking of the drunkard (*Prov.* 23:33). It may be called Gad, for a troop follows it (*Gen.* 30:11). Hence one aptly calls it, *the devil's bridle,* by which he turns the sinner which way he pleases; he that is overcome by it, can overcome no other sin.

But if none of the former considerations can prevail, I hope these two last may, unless all sense and tenderness be lost. Consider, therefore, in the 9th place,

ARGUMENT 9.

That drunkards are in Scripture marked out for hell; the characters of death are upon them.

You shall find them pinioned with other sons of death:

Know ye not that the unrighteous shall not inherit the kingdom of God? Be not deceived: Neither fornicators, nor idolaters, nor adulterers, nor effeminate, nor abusers of themselves with mankind, nor thieves, nor covetous, nor drunkards, nor revilers, nor extortioners, shall inherit the kingdom of God (1 *Cor.* 6:9-10).

Oh dreadful thunder-bolt! He is not *asleep* but *dead*, that is not startled at it.

Lord, how are guilty sinners able to face such a text as this is! Oh soul!—do you dare for a superfluous cup, adventure to drink a cup of pure unmixed wrath? O think when the wine sparkles in the glass, and gives its colour, think, I say, what a cup of trembling is in the hand of the Lord for you. You will not now believe this. Oh! but the day is coming, when you shall know the price of these brutish pleasures. Oh! it will then sting like an adder, Ah! this short-lived beastly pleasure is the price for which you sell heaven, and rivers of pleasure that are at God's right hand.

OBJECTION.

But I hope I shall repent; and then this text can be no bar to my salvation.

SOLUTION.

True; if God shall give you repentance, it could not. But, in the last place, to awaken you thoroughly, and startle your secure conscience, which sensuality has brawned and cauterized, let me tell you,—

ARGUMENT 10.

That it is a sin out of whose power few, or none are ever rescued and reclaimed.

On this account it was that Augustine called it the *pit of hell*. He that is addicted to this sin becomes incurable, says a reverend divine; for seldom or never have I known a drunkard reclaimed. And its power to hold the soul in subjection to it, lies in two things especially:

(1.) As it becomes habitual; and habits are not easily broken.

Be pleased to view an example in the case, Proverbs 23:35: 'They have stricken me, shalt thou say, and I was not sick; they have beaten me, and I felt it not. When shall I awake? I will seek it yet again.'

(2.) As it 'takes away the heart', (*Hos.* 4:11), that is, the understanding, reason, and ingenuity of a man, and so makes him incapable of being reclaimed by counsel.

Upon this account it was that Abigail would not speak less or more to Nabal, until the wine was gone out of him, (1 *Sam.* 25:36-37). Plainly intimating, that no wholesome counsel can get in until the wine be gone out. When one asked Cleostratus, whether he were not ashamed to be drunk, he tartly replied, 'And are not you ashamed to admonish a drunkard?' Intimating that no wise man would cast away an admonition upon such an one. And it not only renders them incapable of counsel for the time, but by degrees it besots and infatuates them; which is a very grievous stroke from God upon them, making way to their eternal ruin.

So then you see upon the whole what a dangerous gulf the sin of drunkenness is. I beg you, for the Lord's sake, and by all the regard you have to your souls, bodies, and estates, beware of it. O consider these ten arguments I have here produced against it. I should have proceeded to answer the several pleas and excuses you have for it; but I mind brevity, and shall shut up this first caution with a very pertinent and ingenious poem of Mr George Herbert, in his *Temple*.

Drink not the third glass, which thou canst not tame
  When once it is within thee; but before
May'st rule it as thou list: and pour the shame
  Which it will pour to thee upon the floor.
  It is most just to throw that on the ground,
  Which would throw me there, if I kept the round.

He that is drunken, may his mother kill,
  Lie with his sister: he hath lost the reins;
Is outlaw'd by himself; all kind of ill
  Did with the liquor slide into the veins.
  The drunkard forfeits man, and doth divest
  All worldly right, save what he has by beast.

Shall I, to please another's wine-sprung mind,
  Lose all my own? God has given me a measure
Short of his Can, and body; must I find
  A pain in that wherein he finds a pleasure?
  Stay at the third glass; if thou lose thy hold,
  Then thou art modest, but the wine grows bold,

If reason move not gallants quit the room,
  (All in a shipwreck shift their several way.)
Let not a common ruin thee intomb :
  Be not a beast in courtesies; but stay,
  Stay at the third glass, or forego the place:
  Wine, above all things, doth God's stamp deface.

The following short piece, on the evils of drunkenness, has been taken from *John Ploughman's Pictures; or, More of His Plain Talk for Plain People*, by C. H. Spurgeon.

He has a Hole under His Nose
and
His Money Runs into It

This is the man who is always dry, because he takes so much heavy wet. He is a loose fellow who is fond of getting tight. He is no sooner up than his nose is in the cup, and his money begins to run down the hole which is just under his nose. He is not a blacksmith, but he has a spark in his throat, and all the publican's barrels can't put it out. If a pot of beer is a yard of land, he must have swallowed more acres than a ploughman could get over for many a day, and still he goes on swallowing until he takes to wallowing. All goes down Gutter Lane. Like the snipe, he lives by suction. If you ask him how he is, he says he would be quite right if he could moisten his mouth. His purse is a bottle, his bank is the publican's till, and his casket is a cask: pewter is his precious metal, and his purl[3] is a mixture of gin and beer. The dew of his youth comes from Ben Nevis, and the comfort of his soul

---

[3] 'purl': ale warmed and spiced, *Ed.*

is cordial gin. He is a walking barrel, a living drainpipe, a moving swill-tub. They say 'loathe to drink and loathe to leave off', but he never needs persuading to begin, and as to ending—that is out of the question while he can borrow two-pence. This is the gentleman who sings—

> He that buys land buys many stones,
> He that buys meat buys many bones,
> He that buys eggs buys many shells,
> He that buys good ale buys nothing else.

He will never be hanged for leaving his drink behind him. He drinks in season and out of season: in summer because he is hot, and in winter because he is cold. A drop of beer never comes too soon, and he would get up in the middle of the night for more, only he goes to bed too tipsy. He has heard that if you get wet-footed a glass of whisky in your boots will keep you from catching cold, and he argues that the best way to get one glass of the spirit into each boot is to put two doses where it will run into your legs. He is never long without an excuse for another pot, or if perchance he does not make one, another lushington[4] helps him.

Some drink when friends step in,
And some when they step out;
Some drink because they're thin,
And some because they're stout.

Some drink because 'tis wet,
And some because 'tis dry;
Some drink another glass
To wet the other eye.

---

[4] 'lushington': from 'lush': archaic slang for liquor: a drinking bout; a drinker or drunkard, someone who attends a lush-house, a low public house, *Ed.*

Water is this gentleman's abhorrence, whether used inside or out, but most of all he dreads it taken inwardly, except with spirits, and then the less the better. He says that the pump would kill him, but he never gives it a chance. He laps his liquor, and licks his chaps, but he will never die through the badness of the water from the well. It is a pity that he does not run the risk. Drinking cold water neither makes a man sick, nor in debt, nor his wife a widow, but this mighty fine ale of his will do all this for him, make him worse than a beast while he lives, and wash him away to his grave before his time. The old Scotchman said, 'Death and drink-draining axe near neighbours', and he spoke the truth. They say that drunkenness makes some men fools, some beasts, and some devils, but according to my mind it makes all men fools whatever else it does. Yet when a man is as drunk as a rat he sets up to be a judge, and mocks at sober people. Certain neighbours of mine laugh at me for being a teetotaller, and I might well laugh at them for being drunk, only I feel more inclined to cry that they should be such fools. O that we could get them sober, and then perhaps we might make men of them. You cannot do much with these fellows, unless you can enlist them in the Coldstream Guards.

He that any good would win
At his mouth must first begin.

As long as drink drowns conscience and reason, you might as well talk to the hogs. The rascals will promise fair and take the pledge, and then take their coats to pledge to get more beer. We smile at a tipsy man, for he is a ridiculous creature, but when we see how he is ruined body and soul it is no joking matter. How solemn is he truth that 'No drunkard shall inherit eternal life.'

There's nothing too bad for a man to say or do when he is half-seas over. It is a pity that any decent body should go near such a common sewer. If he does not fall into the worst of crimes it certainly is not his fault, for he has made himself ready for anything the devil likes to put into his mind. He does least hurt when he begins to be top-heavy, and to reel about: then he becomes a blind man with good eyes in his head, and a cripple with legs on. He sees two moons, and two doors to the public-house, and tries to find his way through both the doors at once. Over he goes, and there he must lie unless somebody will wheel him home in a barrow or carry him to the police-station.

Solomon says the glutton and the drunkard shall come to poverty, and that the drinker does in no time. He gets more and more down at the heel, and as his nose gets redder and his body is more swollen he gets to be more of a shack and more of a shark. His trade is gone, and his credit has run out, but he still manages to get his beer. He treats an old friend to a pot, and then finds that he has left his purse at home, and of course the old friend must pay the shot. He borrows till no one will lend him a groat, unless it is to get off lending a shilling. Shame has long since left him, though all who know him are ashamed of him. His talk runs like the tap, and is full of stale dregs: he is very kind over his beer, and swears he loves you, and would like to drink your health, and love you again. Poor sot, much good will his blessing do to any one who gets it; his poor wife and family have had too much of it already, and quake at the very sound of his voice.

Now, if we try to do anything to shut up a boozing-house, or shorten the hours for guzzling, we are called all sorts of bad names, and the wind-up of it all is—*'What! Rob a poor man of his beer?'* The fact is that they rob the poor man by his beer. The ale-jug robs the cupboard and the table, starves the wife and strips the children; it is a great thief, housebreaker, and heartbreaker, and the best possible thing is to break it to pieces, or keep it on the shelf bottom upwards.

In a newspaper which was lent me the other day I saw some verses by John Barley-corn, Jun., and as they tickled my fancy I copied them out, and here they are.

What! rob a poor man of his beer,
And give him good victuals instead!
Your heart's very hard, sir, I fear,
Or at least you are soft in the head.

What! rob a poor man of his mug,
And give him a house of his own;
With kitchen and parlour so snug!
'Tis enough to draw tears from a stone.

What! rob a poor man of his glass,
And teach him to read and to write!
What! save him from being an ass!
'Tis nothing but malice and spite.

What! rob a poor man of his ale,
And prevent him from beating his wife,
From being locked up in a jail,
With penal employment for life!

What! rob a poor man of his beer,
And keep him from starving his child!
It makes one feel awfully queer,
And I'll thank you to draw it more mild.

Having given you a song, I now hand
you a handbill to stick up in the 'Rose and
Crown' window, if the landlord wants an
advertisement. It was written many years
ago, but it is quite as good as new. Any
beer-seller may print it who thinks it likely
to help his trade:

Drunkards, Read This!

DRUNKENNESS

EXPELS REASON,
DISTEMPERS THE BODY,
DIMINISHES STRENGTH,
INFLAMES THE BLOOD;

CAUSES { INTERNAL EXTERNAL ETERNAL INCURABLE } WOUNDS

IS

A WITCH TO THE SENSES,
A DEMON TO THE SOUL,
A THIEF TO THE PURSE,
A GUIDE TO BEGGARY, LECHERY, & VILLAINY.

IT IS

THE WIFE'S WOE, AND
THE CHILDREN'S SORROW.

MAKES A MAN

WALLOW WORSE THAN A BEAST, AND
ACT LIKE A FOOL.

HE IS

A SELF-MURDERER;
WHO DRINKS TO ANOTHER'S GOOD HEALTH,

AND

ROBS HIMSELF OF HIS OWN

OTHER BOOKS IN THE
POCKET PURITANS
SERIES

Anger Management Richard Baxter
Heaven, a World of Love Jonathan Edwards
Impure Lust John Flavel
Living Faith Samuel Ward
The Loveliness of Christ Samuel Rutherford (gift ed.)
Repent and Believe Thomas Brooks
Sinful Speech John Flavel
Truth For All Time John Calvin (gift ed.)

If you enjoyed reading this little book then you may
be interested to know that the Banner of Truth Trust
also publishes the six-volume set of Flavel's *Works*
(ISBN: 978 0 85151 060 6, approximately 600 pp.
per volume, clothbound), and Flavel's *The Mystery of
Providence* (ISBN: 978 0 85151 104 7, 224pp. paperback) in the Puritan Paperback series.

For more details of these and all other Banner
of Truth titles, please visit our website:
www.banneroftruth.co.uk

Some Reviews of Flavel's Works

―――――――

Flavel's work includes catchy titles, striking sayings, apt quotations, and simple illustrations. We know a pastor who has profited greatly from reading a sermon or chapter of Flavel every morning for decades. When he finishes volume 6, the pastor begins over again with volume 1. If you can afford only a few sets of Puritan works, Flavel's should be included.

Tolle Lege
Reformation Heritage Books Catalogue

It is the considered opinion of your reviewer that here in these volumes both ministers and laity alike will find a feast of good things. Flavel's sermons are not long, but they are models of exposition and application. Preachers particularly will find useful topics, sermon-series and other valuable aids, not least of which will be Flavel's analysis of spiritual conditions. All his writings are scripturally based. These well bound, clear-printed volumes are at a price amazingly small for such a treasury of Puritan spirituality . . . To buy the works of Flavel is an investment and not an expense, for to the buyer there will be found a rich return for a lifetime and beyond.

ENGLISH CHURCHMAN

D. Martyn Lloyd-Jones on Flavel

John Flavel [1628-1691], son of a Puritan minister who died in prison for his Nonconformity, was educated at University College, Oxford, and laboured for almost the entire period of his ministry at Dartmouth, Devon. Having all the characteristics of the tradition to which he belonged—a tradition which believed that preaching should be 'hissing hot', searching and expository—Flavel attained to pre-eminence in his ability to combine both instruction and an appeal to the heart. Some Puritans might be more learned than he, and some more quaint, but for all-round usefulness none was his superior.

The repeated editions of Flavel bear their own witness to his poularity: five times were his Collected Works issued in the 18th cen-

tury and at least three times in the 19th. He was a favourite with Jonathan Edwards and George Whitefield [who ranked him with John Bunyan and Matthew Henry], and a century later, with such Scottish evangelical leaders as R. M. M'Cheyne and Andrew Bonar. But it was in the homes of Christian people that Flavel made his greatest appeal and influenced rising generations. Archibald Alexander, the first professor at Princeton Seminary, read him while still a 'teenager' and recorded later in life, 'To John Flavel I certainly owe more than to any uninspired author.'

His six volumes are in themselves a library of the best Puritan divinity and a set will be a life-long treasure to those who possess it. He is one of that small number of evangelical writers who can by their lucidity and simplicity help those at the beginning of the

Christian life and at the same time be a strong companion to those who near its end.

Having read his work for many years I have always regarded him as one of the warmest and most experimental of the Puritan writers. He is also eminently readable.

THE
POCKET PURITANS
SERIES

To read the work of a Puritan doctor of the soul is to enter a rich world of spiritual theology to feed the mind, heart-searching analysis to probe the conscience, Christ-centred grace to transform the heart, and wise counsel to direct the life. This series of Pocket Puritans provides all this in miniature, but also in abundance.

SINCLAIR B. FERGUSON

THE BANNER OF TRUTH TRUST

3 Murrayfield Road,
Edinburgh EH12 6EL
UK

P O Box 621, Carlisle,
Philadelphia 17013,
USA

www.banneroftruth.co.uk